RASPBERRY Pi 4
BEGINNER'S GUIDE

The Complete User Manual for Beginners to Set
up Innovative Projects on Raspberry Pi 4
(2020 Edition)

LOUIS

GOMERA

Copyright © 2020 Louis Gomera

All rights reserved.

Disclaimer

The information in this book is based on personal experience and anecdotal evidence. Although the author has made every attempt to achieve an accuracy of the information gathered in this book, they make no representation or warranties concerning the accuracy or completeness of the contents of this book. Your circumstances may not be suited to some illustrations in this book.

The author disclaims any liability arising directly or indirectly from the use of this book. Readers are encouraged to seek accounting, legal, or professional help when required.

This guide is for informational purposes only, and the author does not accept any responsibilities for any liabilities resulting from the use of this information. While every attempt has been made to verify the information provided here, the author cannot assume any responsibility for errors, inaccuracies, or omission.

Printed in the United States of America

TABLE OF CONTENTS

INTRODUCTION

Raspberry Pi and versions that
followed after it has revolutionized
computing because of its size,
capability, and price that has
attracted many people who hitherto
were unable to own a computer
system because of the high cost of
acquiring one. Designed initially like
Dell in terms of low cost, to bring the
cost of acquiring a PC to the lowest
ebb, so that people all over the
world, particularly Africa, can also

Have the opportunity to buy. Also, it was invented as a supportive aid to learning computer programming, gaming consoles, and other educational purposes. The idea was conceived by the UK based Raspberry Pi Foundation to be used in teaching basic computer science in schools and developing countries; it has taken users into deferent parts of the computing world.

CHAPTER ONE

What is Raspberry Pi?

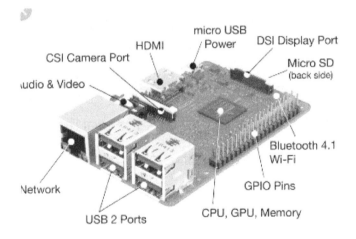

The Raspberry Pi was borne out of the desire by computer gurus at the University of Cambridge Computer

Laboratory to revisit the days when children were playing computer games and programming inexpensive computers. The idea behind the Raspberry Pi was to make computers affordable as far as possible; hence only the basics were offered and is supported with a programming environment and hardware connections for electronic projects. The Raspberry Pi runs on Raspbian (a modified version of Linux), and it is directly on the SD card, which provides a graphical interface for using the operating system. The SD card is also used as terminal apps for gaining entry into the Command line connecting it up.

The Raspberry Pi is offered in both starter kits and a single board, which means that on your own, you can buy all the extras required to make it fully functional. The SD card becomes very important as it acts as the storage for the operating system and any software that can be installed

Raspberry is a desktop computer

The Raspberry P1 has now come up with version 4; it shouldn't be a kid's toy. It's a full-on computer that supports things like 4K video, and it is housed in a credit-card size motherboard that's also well affordable.

The vast majority of users of Raspberry Pi 4 are comfortable using it to do the necessary things desktop computers can do such as word processing, surfing the internet, shopping online, communicating with friends on Facebook, and stream movies and shows.

Your Raspberry Pi 4 can share some of the same components with your smart-phone, and with the software, things couldn't be more different. At the heart of your smartphone is Linux, but Linux has various programs for different uses.

The Linux you can install on a Raspberry Pi is the same as to what you can install on a desktop tower, laptop, or server. In order words, with Raspberry Pi 4, you have access to a desktop-class web browser, photo and video control, and the extent of professional audio production tools, you have them available to install. What cannot be possible, of course, you can even use a Raspberry Pi as a dedicated server for web pages, an FTP host, or a home network file server. All you need to do to begin using Raspberry Pi 4 is the same mouse, keyboard, and monitor you would need for a more traditional desktop and a wall socket to plug everything in.

The Raspberry Pi 4 – what is new?

The Raspberry Pi, 4 Model B, is the latest version in the series of Raspberry Pi computers. The Pi isn't like your usual device; because it comes without a case, and in its cheapest form, it is merely a credit-card sized electronic board – just like the type you find inside a PC or laptop, but the size is much smaller.

What is then new?

• Two display (4K) support: With this feature, it is possible to now connect dual displays to the Raspberry Pi computer, and that also in 4K.

- Guaranteed better performance: The new Raspberry Pi 4 is supplied with a new, modernized processor and higher RAM, which gives you a unique desktop experience.

- Fast internet surfing: The Pi 4 is provided with Gigabit Ethernet, together with onboard wireless networking, including Bluetooth.

- RAM: Raspberry Pi 4 is supplied in RAM: 1 GB, 2 GB, and 4 GB. The choice of what you want is yours.

- USB: The new Raspberry Pi 4 has upgraded USB 3 capacity to two USB 2 ports, this means you will find two USB 3 ports, which is capable of transferring data as much as ten times faster.

Technical specifications

•   Broadcom BCM2711, Quad-core Cortex-A72 (ARM v8) 64-bit SoC @ 1.5GHz

•   4GB, 2GB or 1GB LPDDR4-2400 SDRAM (this is model dependent)

•   2.4 GHz and 5.0 GHz IEEE 802.11ac wireless, BLEGB Ethernet2 USB 3.0 ports; 2 USB 2.0 ports, Bluetooth 5.00

•   Raspberry Pi standard 40 pin GPIO header (compatible with previous boards)

•   2-lane MIPI DSI display port

- 2-lane MIPI CSI camera port

- 2 × micro-HDMI ports (up to 4kp60 supported)

- 4-pole stereo audio and composite video port

- H.265 (4kp60 decode), H264 (1080p60 decode, 1080p30 encode)

- Open GL ES 3.0 graphics

- Micro-SD card slot for loading operating system and used for storing data

- 5V DC through USB-C connector (minimum 3A*)

- 5V DC through GPIO header (minimum 3A*)

•	The power within Ethernet (PoE) enabled (doesn't require separate PoE HAT)

•	A good quality 2.5A power supply can be appropriate if downstream USB peripherals consume less than 500mA in total.

CHAPTER TWO

Setting up your Raspberry Pi 4

What you will need

A power supply: A USB Type-C port supplied with the device. You need a power supply of 3.00 least 3.0 A power.

Micro-SD card: You will need a formatted Micro SD card to enable files to be stored and the Raspbian Operating System. 8 GB is the minimum storage requirement, but you need more than 8 GB. You may have your Raspberry Pi 4 pre-installed with the Raspberry Operating System, so you are ready to start using the system.

Keyboard and mouse: These are mandatory if you want to start using the Raspberry Pi 4. Both are compulsory for the first installation. After the initial set up, you can also use Bluetooth keyboard and mouse if you wish.

TV/Computer screen: For the content inside the computer to be displayed, you need a TV or computer screen, and a cable to link Raspberry and the display. If speakers are pre-installed in it, Pi 4 will use it. The micro-HDMI is the port that is required here unless you have a different cable like standard HDMI, DVI, and VGA cable, and then you will need their respective micro-HDMI converters. For example, if your monitor holds up VGA, then get a VGA-to-micro-HDMI adapter instead. If this is the case, then you will be able to use your VGA cable.

The above are the requirements before setting up the Raspberry Pi 4.

Setting up the SD card

If your SD card is not pre-installed with the Raspbian operating system, you can install it yourself. All you have to do is to make use of a laptop with an installed SD card slot. The latest laptops in the market are included with this feature.

Download Raspbian OS via NOOBS

Using NOOBS to mount the Raspbian operating system is the easiest way to go about the installation.

Steps to download and transfer NOOBS to the micro-SD card

Go to the Raspberry download page and then click on the box which has NOOBS printed on it. It is simpler to download the ZIP file but be sure you know where the file is going to be stored or located so that you will be able to find it in the future when you need it.

Procedure:

•   Use a formatted SD card. If you have other files on it, back them up, then proceed.

•   It is time to extract the files from the ZIP file you have downloaded from NOOBS.

•   It is necessary to open another Explorer window and then navigate to the SD card.

•   Select all the files you want first and then copy all of them for onward pasting into the SD card file.

• Now navigate to your SD card folder, and paste all of it in your micro-SD card.

• Now you can remove the micro-SD card.

This is the time to connect the Raspberry Pi 4

Install all the components necessary into the mini device. You must do the set up in a particular order to safeguard the components.

First of all, plug in the micro-SD card on the underside slot of the Raspberry Pi 4. Get the USB port of your mouse cable, and hook it up to the USB port on Raspberry Pi 4

Hook up the keyboard in the same way. Don't forget to plug in your screen into a socket and turn it ON.

Then hook up the TV/computer monitor to your device using a micro-HDMI cable, or an adapter if necessary.

Place in the slot micro-HDMI female part into the port named HDMI0 in Raspberry Pi.

To hook up Raspberry Pi 4 to the web via Ethernet, connect an Ethernet cable linked to a Wi-Fi router or a broadband connection. If your screen has speakers fixed in it, the Raspberry Pi will make use of those. If you want to do away with those speakers or no speakers are connected to your monitor, you can connect external speakers like headphones or by connecting them through a headphone jack.

Booting the Raspberry Pi 4

The Raspberry Pi computer doesn't have a power button, so as soon as you connect the power supply and turn it on, it boots up immediately.

You should notice the red LED light gleaming in the device. This is evidence that Raspberry is connected to power. In a moment, as the booting up is in progress, raspberries on the left of your screen will be displayed.

After a few seconds, the Raspbian desktop will show up.

Finishing the setup

When the Raspberry Pi 4 is started for the first time, the Welcome to Raspberry Pi will pop-up. This becomes your guide to the initial setup.

Click "Next" to begin the setup. First, set the country you are in, the language, and the time zone. Then, click "Next" again. Type a new password. Hook up to a WiFi network by choosing a name and typing in the password. Permit the wizard check and download updates if there are any, and install them. This may take some time to complete. Click Done or Reboot to finish the setup.

Connecting your Pi 4 to a network

Connecting your Raspberry Pi 4 to the Web is relatively easy.

First, you can connect the Ethernet cable into it, and also you can connect to a wireless network.

Connecting to a wireless network

- Locate the wireless network in the top right-hand of the screen and click on it.

- Select the network you want from the drop-down menu.
- Key in your password for the network, then click **OK**
- A wireless LAN symbol will show up, at once your Pi is hooked up to the internet.

CHAPTER THREE

Choosing an operating system

The Raspberry Pi has attracted a lot of people, far and wide since its inception in 2012. A lot of projects have been executed using Raspberry Pi by the ever-growing community of Raspberry fans. The sky is the limit of what use that can be put to of both the hardware and software of Raspberry Pi. It is capable of running different Linux operating systems. These are known as distributions or distro for short, and can be varied as the number of the projects Raspberry Pi has executed; each project offers a different look and feels, at the same time different functionality. Let us see a range of the best distro that are today available for your Pi.

i.   **Raspbian OS**

Raspbian is the number one of the distro every new user of Raspberry Pi should get hold of. It is supported by Debian Linux, and it is fully optimized for the Raspberry Pi hardware, and it is an ideal starting point, especially for a beginner since it is pre-installed with programs you will need to be up and running. The Raspbian iOS is specially designed and developed for Raspberry Pi. It is ideally appropriate to the limited system resources of the Raspberry Pi.

Raspbian was specially packaged for educational purposes as dictated by the Raspberry Pi Foundation. In the package, you will see programs such as Scratch, which comprises child-friendly graphical beginner programming language whereby games can be created.

ii.   **Arch Linux OS**

Arch is also a Linux distro that has remained available for the past 14 years. It is an excellent operating system that prides itself on its simplicity, code accuracy, and smartness. The port for the Raspberry Pi Arch Linux ARM is geared towards simplicity and gives full control of the operating system to the user. It boots fast to a command prompt, and it is also very light in resource usage. Though its design is more on the user control, very unfriendly to a beginner, compared to the Raspbian

iii.   **Ubuntu MATE and Snappy Core OS**

Ubuntu is like Raspbian, one of the most acclaimed Linux distros for regular desktop and laptop computers. It is very simple to use;

just like Raspbian, it leans heavily on its parent company Canonical. It is offered in two variants – Ubuntu MATE and Snappy Ubuntu Core. Ubuntu MATE is the common Ubuntu but designed with a different desktop environment. It utilizes the popular MATE desktop instead of the Canonical own Unity desktop. Snappy Ubuntu Core is a stripped-own version of the operating system that is based on transactional updates; it is designed to run on the Internet of Things (IoT) devices. You can have a look at it if you are designing a product to be powered by the Raspberry Pi.

iv.   **OSMC and OpenELEC OS**

Many people that operate their Raspberry Pi use it as media servers. This is a device to connect to hook up to your home network that can relay music to the house.

Installing the Operating System (OS)

One of the primary objectives of the Pi was to increase computer literacy level, particularly at a lower income level, instead of learning how to set up a database, the Pi has many other uses. Pi is essentially a mini-computer with HDMI and analog TV output; it can carry out many other tasks that are common to a laptop or desktop.

There is a wide range of OS explicitly optimized for the Pi, the most popular is the Raspbian, which is a port of Debian. Debian is a key part of the Linux ecosystem, including other popular open-source distributions, which are pronged from the Debian source code.

Having assembled all the required hardware, it is now time to install the operating system. Irrespective of the project you are in, the procedure for installing the operating system is generally the same. Unlike the traditional PC, which has BIOS, a drive that supports CD or DVD, with a hard disk inside the PC, the Raspberry Pi has a card reader. In this case, you must follow a different set-up route of inserting a boot disk and installing your operating system to an internal storage device

How to install an OS

- Obtaining the OS
The Pi OS can be obtained from the main Raspberry site, from where it can be downloaded. On the OS download page, you will discover NOOBS. You download it and then unzip the files to a freshly formatted SD

card and follow the on-screen instructions.

- Find within the zip file, a file with a img or iso extension. Extract the file and copy it to a formatted SD card.

- Insert your SD card in the Pi and start it up. You are starting up your Pi for the first time, so attach all the necessary cables and peripherals to your Raspberry Pi. It is only the power cable that is left behind. Gently insert the SD card in the slot. Wait for the SD card to be seated firmly, plug the micro USB power cable. You must realize that there is no power button on the Pi, so once you plug in the power cable, the booting process will begin. A few seconds later, the booting will be completed.

Discover the best apps for Raspberry Pi

Since Raspberry Pi is a Linux-based computer, it means you can run Linux programs on your Raspberry Pi. The only thing you have to do is to check the software requirements and be sure that the selected software meets the recommended minimum specifications.

Here are some of the most important software you can install onto your Raspberry Pi.

- **Libre-Office**

  This is the best office application suite that is compatible with the Microsoft office. It is capable of fulfilling all the data processing tasks.

- **Node-RED**

  This program was put together by software experts at IBM. The apps use a graphical interface to drag, drop, and link different elements, making it possible for you to program and hook up together internet of Things devices.

- **Chromium**

    This is a web browser that is related to the well-known Google Chrome. Chrome add-ons can be installed on these apps, such as Google Hangouts plug-in from the Google web store.

- **Deluge (Download files through Bit BitTorrent)**

    Deluge is one of the best apps for downloading files via Bit Torrent. If you operate your Pi without a monitor, you can access Deluge via a web interface from another device. This is very useful if you away from your home base.

- **Synaptic Package Manager**
This application is the equivalent of Add/Remove Software. The good thing about Synaptic is that if you choose an app for installation that requires other subprograms to function correctly, it will select the programs for download as well.

- **Owncloud**
Owncloud means that you don't need to store your files in a Dropbox or similar online storage facility but you create

your online storage facility.
Once fully operational, it will
monitor up-dates from installed
programs and alert you once
up-dates are available.

- **Pidgin (Manage all your Messaging from one place)**
Pidgin is a cross-platform
messaging app that will save
you the trouble of managing
multiple accounts. All your
chats can be pooled together
in one place.

- **Nagiospi**
This software boots your security
by monitoring your home and
internet security for some
unseemly web traffic

- **SD Card Copier**

  Your valuable photos,
  messages, emails, maybe
  precious to you that you want
  reliable backup storage. Even
  though there are other
  available means of keeping this
  date, the build-in SD Card
  Copier is one of the most
  reliable.

Install and use packages

If you are not conversant with Linux,
you may discover that its built-in APT
package management tool is a bit
scary and tricky to catch up with.

The APT-Get command is the package installer via the internet, which connects to the remote servers. However, it is used via the terminal command prompt, which makes it a bit complex to use, so an alternative must be found; a desktop environment interface method of holding packages.

Using applications

i.   Stop motion camera

Creating your digital stop motion camera, you should have a Raspberry Pi 4 and a devoted camera component. The procedure for creating a camera is lengthy and takes time to complete. You definitely will need Python, a camera with a tripod, and a well-lit area, a breadboard to mount a button, (unless there is an alternative such as a suitable plunger button to be connected to the Raspberry Pi's GPIO) and a Python script to take each picture.

ii. Webserver

It is now possible to put together your Raspberry Pi 4 to host a website and a blog. You can do it in one of two ways: You can either mount an Apache and its related files or mount a full LAMP stack, with

PHP and MYSQL together with Apache. Configuring the FPT is suitable.

As soon as you are through with either of the two, you can bring in HTML files into the \www\ directory. You also have the option of installing a specific website like the Word Press, and your web server is ready. To bring the website online, you will need to contact your Internet Service Provider for a static IP address.

iii. **Network monitoring tool**

The network monitoring tool monitors devices on the network, especially if you are concerned about a lack of connectivity. If you want to create a network monitoring tool out of the available tools, Nagios is considered the best since it is easy to set up and operate.

Once you set up the Nagios tool, you can easily monitor up time and visualize the devices connected. To use the Nagios tool, you will have to flash the disk image to the SD card already installed in your Raspberry Pi 4.

iv. **Stream live video to YouTube**

This is another way to make use of Pi 4 to take advantage of installed applications. To live stream to YouTube, you must have a compatible USB camera.

v. Study how to code

Coding was one of the primary objectives of inventing this device, to teach children how to code. However, adults can also learn the coding system too, making use of the in-build coding tools available on the Raspberry Pi 4.

Basic programming skills can be learned using many pieces of software available in Raspbian. The most important to use is Scratch.

Scratch is made to cater to all levels, and it is a block-based programming tool. It avoids the complicated part of imputing lines of code. In its place, you drag a command into place, view the impact of the command, and exporting the code as a program to run.

Scratch is a straightforward tool to use; it can manipulate lights installed in the Pi's GPIO and can program basic games.

CHAPTER FOUR

Features of Raspberry Pi 4

The Raspberry Pi 4 computer systems have many new features, making it a perfect choice for a variety of projects. This book will show you the features of the Pi 4 to include, what projects it can be good at, and how it is different from earlier versions of Raspberry Pi computers.

The Raspberry Pi 4, similar to its prior versions, is an ARM-based single-board computer that includes a 1.5GHz 64-bit quad-core ARM Cortex

CUP, on-board wireless LAN, USB, GPIO, display port, and Ethernet. But in contrast with its previous versions, the Raspberry Pi 4 comes with a variety of new features to significantly boost the maker field, at the same time, offer users a wide range of choices when it comes to programming. The Raspberry Pi 4 is provided with three variants of RAM, including 1GB, 2GB, and 4GB. The Pi also is offered with two devoted micro HDMI ports, letting for multi-screen function, on-board Bluetooth 5.0, gigabit Ethernet, as well as two USB 3.0 ports for fast data transmission. The power port to the Pi altered via using a USB B Micro connector to a USB-C power connector, which indicates that users shouldn't forget to have a USB-C type cable handy

Differences in Pi

A lot of differences are now visible. One of the mainly distinguishable differences between the Raspberry Pi 3 B+ and Raspberry Pi 4 is the updated CPU, from an A53 to an A72. This significant update, according to a statement released by the Raspberry Pi Foundation, can offer users with up to three times the performance of the earlier version. Moreover, the Raspberry Pi 4 has broader available RAM options, letting users have more flexibility in option when crafting an application with the Pi in mind.

The Pi 4 also offers users with twin display ports instead for multi-screen operation and the choice of 4K resolution at 60 frames in one second on one screen or 4K resolution at 30 frames in one second on two screens

Practical Applications of the Raspberry Pi 4

•   With an enhanced core, enlarged RAM, and superior performance GPU, the practical applications of the Raspberry Pi 4 have significantly expanded.

Besides, the Raspberry Pi 4 is capable of running nearly all projects more efficiently, but the addition of twin monitors, enlarged RAM, and processor swiftness is particularly helpful for AI and machine education projects. By employing the use of USB 3.0 ports and gigabit Ethernet also contribute to making the Raspberry Pi 4 far more appropriate as a networked device than its earlier versions, making it a perfect network storage space and web host. Moreover, the use of low-energy Bluetooth 5 lets the Raspberry Pi hook up to the vast majority of Bluetooth devices together with pointing devices, speakers, and sensors. If we put together the wireless capability of the Pi 4, included with its network capacity and ability to execute machine learning algorithms, then the Pi 4 qualifies to become the ideal home automation applications requiring machine control over LAN, interpreting wireless sensors and identifying user's movement around a room or property.

Projects with the New Pi 4

Although it may not display every project, the Raspberry Pi 4 can create, this list offers quite a few examples of what New Pi can be employed to do.

- Network Drive – Fast USB 3.0 port and the Ethernet capacity

- Home Automation – This can include facial identification and wireless connectivity

- Data Monitoring Station – Twin screen maintenance for enlarged data showing

- Automated Security System – this uses facial recognition

- Web Host – High-speed USB 3.0 port, high processing capacity, and Ethernet connectivity

- Network Drive – Fast USB 3.0 port and the Ethernet capacity

- Networked Device / IoT

- Remote measurement

- Object recognition + sorting

- Robotic Arm

- Remote measurement

- Automated placement system

- IIoT Device

CHAPTER FIVE

Powering the Board

Another big difference introduced with Raspberry Pi 4 is the power jack, with the exit of the micro USB jack from previous models, and now replaced with a USB-C jack. It's an agreeable change. The endurances on the power supply for the Raspberry Pi 3, Model B+ were already at the breaking point, with the new board needing up to 3 Amps, it has become obvious that the previous micro USB would not be able to supply it.

The board can also be powered through 5V DC supply using the GPIO headers, and compared with the Raspberry Pi 3, Model B+, before it, the new Raspberry Pi 4 can also be power-driven by Power Over Ethernet (PoE) via the official PoE HAT that was released together with the previous model the year before.

A Fresh Official Power Supply

With the change from micro USB to USB-C, a new official power supply is introduced. However, while USB-C chargers usually sell within the range of between $10 and $60, the new 15W official power supply is retail at just $8, which is knock off price. A lot of potential buyers that are yet to hear about Raspberry Pi will buy it at that price point. Moreover, unlike the original micro USB supply was designed as a power supply, the new USB-C power supply has been designed as a power supply, and not a charger.

The power supply feature is a big difference.

Programming for beginners

Using Raspberry Pi 4 is using software created by other people; in this part of the article, it's about creating your program, based on what you think you want to do. You can create your program whether you have previous experience or not; you are going to use a process known as programming or coding, and you'll find the Raspberry Pi an excellent platform for this creative work and experimentation of the program.

The key to accessing the coding on the Pi is Scratch; it is a visual programming language. In the same way, the traditional programming language has been text-based written as instructions for the computer to carry out, the same way you might write a recipe for cooking fried rice. Scratch will help you build your program step-by-step via blocks – pre-written chunks of code hidden behind color-coded

Jigsaw pieces.

Scratch is, therefore, a great first language for budding coders for everyone, but don't be tricked by its pleasant appearance: it's a dominant and fully well-designed programming environment for creating everything from simple games and animations through to complex interactive robotics projects.

Introducing the Scratch 2 interface

Stage Area – Like actors in a play, your nymphs move around the stage under the
control of your program.

Sprite – The characters or things you control in a Scratch program are known
as sprites, and assemble on the stage.

Stage Controls – Your stage can be re-arranged, with adding your images as backgrounds, using the stage controls.

Sprites List – All the sprites you have produced and loaded into Scratch will show
in this section of the window.

Blocks Palette – All the blocks available for your program become visible in the blocks palette, which features color-coded groupings.

Blocks – Pre-written chunks of program code blocks let you assemble your program step-by-step.

Scripts Area – The scripts area is where your program is constructed by drawing-and- placing blocks from the blocks palette.

Your first Scratch program: Hello, All

Scratch 2 loads most program on the Pi: click on the Raspberry logo to load the

Raspbian menu, navigate to the Programming section, and click on Scratch 2.

After a moment, the Scratch 2 user interface will load and show on the screen.

The vast majority of programming languages need you to tell the computer what to do via written instructions; Scratch does its own differently. Begin by clicking on the Looks group in the blocks palette, located in the center of the Scratch window. This calls up the blocks under that group, colored purple. Locate the say, Hello! Block, click and hold the left mouse button on it, and draw it across to the scripts area at the right-hand side of the Scratch window, after which you let go the mouse button

Python programming

Python is based on text: you note down instructions, using a simple English language and specific format, the computer then carries out the task.

Python is a leap forward to those who are already conversant with Scratch, making programming more flexible in a more 'traditional' programming environment. That does not mean it's not difficult to learn, but with a little practice, anyone can be used to writing Python programs for almost everything from simple text through to startlingly complicated calculations.

This chapter continues from the terms and concepts introduced in Programming with

Scratch. If you are yet to work through the exercises in the previous chapter yet, you'll follow this chapter with ease if you go back and do so first.

Your first Python program: Hello, World!

Like the other pre-installed programs on the Raspberry Pi, this is available from the menu: click on the Raspberry logo, navigate to the Programming section, and click on

Thonny Python IDE. After a moment, the Thonny user interface will load and appear on the screen.

Thonny is a package known as an integrated development environment (IDE), a name that means: it brings together, or assembles, all the different tools you need to write or build-up program into a single user interface. There are so many IDEs on hand, many of which hold up many diverse programming languages while others, like Thonny focal point, is on supporting a single language.

Unlike Scratch, which provides you with visual building blocks as a source for your program, Python is a more conventional encoding language where everything is in writing.

Begin your first program when you click on the Python shell area at the bottom-left of the Thonny window, then type this instruction: print("Hello, World!"), and then press the ENTER key:

Once you press the ENTER key, you'll see that your program starts to run right away: In the shell area, you will see Python respond, with the message 'Hello, World!' the same way you have asked. The reason for that is because the shell is a direct line to the Python interpreter, whose work it is to find your instructions and interpret it to the letter. We call this interactive mode, and you can imagine it like an in-person conversation with someone: once you finish what you're saying, the other person will act in response, then wait for what you are going to say next.

CHAPTER SIX

Raspberry Pi 4 performance

Raspberry Pi 4 is undoubtedly the next generation Pi, with two screen 4k support, USB 3.0, brand new CPU and GPU, and RAMs 1GB, 2GB, and 4GB.

Indeed Raspberry Pi 4 is a huge leap forward to the low-cost computer. They are specially designed to let people experiment with programming and building hardware.

The Raspberry Pi 4 leap to 4GB, support for 4K displays, true GB

Ethernet, the bump in processor speed to 1.5GHz, the addition of USB 3.0, and upgrading to a modern system-on-chip.

Moreover, the ability to run twin displays and still retain the price at which the Pi was fixed since its inception in 2012.

Raspberry Pi 4 is a system of many resources. Leisure driven enthusiasts use Pi boards as file servers, media centers, routers, retro games consoles, and network-level ad-blockers, for beginners. However, that is just the tip of the iceberg. There are so many projects out there, in which people have built tablets with Pi, laptops, phones, robots, smart mirrors, to snap images on the edge of space, and run experiments on the Global Space Station

With the Pi 4 being faster with 4GB, and as a result, able to decode 4K video, benefiting from faster storage through USB 3.0, and quicker network connections via true Gigabit Ethernet. It's also the first Pi that supports dual displays -- up to dual 4K@30 displays -- a big opportunity for creatives who crave for more desktop space.

Raspberry Pi 4 capability

What makes Raspberry Pi 4 different from previous versions?

The Raspberry Pi, 4 Model B, is faster and also more proficient than the ones preceding it, the Raspberry Pi 3 Model B+. For those interested in evaluation, the Pi 4's CPU -- the board's main processor -- is capable of providing two to three times the performance of the Pi3's processor in some aspects of a benchmark.

Unlike its Pi 3 board, the new board is built to playing 4K video at 60 frames per second, enhancing the Pi's media center credentials. That does not mean, however, that all video will scale through smoothly, and sustaining this hardware speeding up for H.265-encoded video is presently a work in progress across the Pi's various operating systems, so this is something expected to take place in the future than is available today.

The Pi 4 also functions with wireless internet out of the box, with built-in Wi-Fi and Bluetooth.

The most recent board is also capable of booting directly from a USB-attached hard drive or a pen drive, and the next future firmware update will boot directly from a network-attached file system using PXE. Supporting a network-connected drive is helpful for distantly updating a Pi and for giving out an OS image between Pi, Pi 2, and Pi 4

The Raspberry Pi 4 and desktop PC

The Pi can be run as a low-cost budget desktop, and with the launching of the Pi 4, it's never been like a PC. The biggest advantage for everyday use is in office apps, web surfing, support for online services -- is the additional space.

With 4GB RAM, the Pi 4 no longer sags as a result of the heavy web pages and apps and is now capable of switching between full online services such as Google's G Suite and today's JavaScript overloaded sites without sagging. In many respects, it feels almost the same with a PC costing much higher in price -- thanks to the improved specs and the small fry yet powerful Raspbian desktop.

Using Raspberry Pi 4

Using Raspberry is not going to be the same thing as a high-end laptop, as it is likened to running a computer on a mobile-targeted processor, but as already been mentioned, how it performs? With the steady progress being made from software to online services, the browser is progressively the only app that a PC needs to run, and based on that; Pi 4 does exceptionally well. Moreover, the extra memory of up to 4GB and the Raspberry Pi Foundation's effort on optimizing Raspbian's default Chromium browser, all add up to the Raspberry Pi 4 performance.

In fact, in the weeks following the Pi 4's launch, the aspects that are behind on the Raspbian desktop be likely to relate to video playback; however, this mapped out to be taken care of by an upcoming software update.

The Pi also works well as a thin-client, as it was found when it was compared with the performance being almost the same with running a modern Windows 10 PC, except for the prolonged transfer of data to USB sticks. This was based on a Pi 3, so a Pi 4 functioning with its true Gigabit Ethernet should perform even better as a thin client.

CHAPTER SEVEN

Surfing the web with
Raspberry Pi 4

Chromium is the official web browser for Raspberry Pi. It starts up quickly on the RPI4, and it's reasonably quick to navigate. Rendering internet pages is slower on the RPI4 than a less well-spaced Chrome book-running Gallium OS. But it's still adequately lively for light to moderate internet browsing. It suffers on web sites much loaded with JavaScript.

Smooth scrolling is enabled by default. Scrolling up and down internet pages in Chromium is not for the most part smooth with a creepy rippling effect evident. It's meant to come alive more smoothly when scrolling pages content. But switching off Smooth Scrolling, the rippling effect is eliminated, and a better scrolling effect is experienced.

There are many options you can set up outside turning off Smooth Scrolling, these are available in chrome://flags.

One way of reducing the rippling effect is to periodically wipe the browser cache One way is to form an alias in ~/.bashrc along the lines of alias clean-chromium-cache=" rm -Rf ~/.cache/chromium/Default/Cache. "

If you do want to clean the cache, just run clean-chromium-cache. Autocomplete will reduce the number of characters you need to input or apply a shorter name for the alias.

Chromium is a memory hog apparently, but that pertains to an Arch Linux box. Even with lots of tabs open, the 4GB RAM model doesn't run into any memory problems. But you'll almost certainly want to use a different web browser if you've got the 1GB model, or you upgrade to Pi 4GB

If you try some activities with Chromium on the RPI4 such as web shopping, reading email via Gmail, accessing Discord servers, and even more, besides. The experience would be quite encouraging. A huge leap compared to its predecessors.

From experience, video streaming with Chromium on the RPI4 is not good enough, given that it is a core activity when web browsing, so it's undoubtedly a sticking point. There is more work to be done on the browser before achieving first-rate video streaming.

Using Raspberry Pi 4 as a media center

Various options are available if you want to use the Pi 4 as a media center, and the most popular choices are the Kodi-based OSes OSMC or LibreElec.

The Pi 4 has the added benefit of being a faster and newer CPU and graphics processor, which the Raspberry Pi Foundation has recommended should be able to play local H.265-encoded video recorded at 3840 x 2160 resolution and 60 frames per second --

Nevertheless, support for this speeding up is still being experimented across the Pi's operating systems. Another benefit is the built-in support for Wi-Fi, which makes it simpler to download content to the Pi, while native Bluetooth makes things easier for hooking up peripherals

Running Raspberry Pi 4 on PS1, NES, SNES, N64, and console games

There are a broad range of classic games that will run on the Pi with the assistance of emulators like RetroPie, as well as some games from all of the systems mentioned above, although the more recent the system, the more likely it is that more severe titles will struggle

Running Raspberry Pi 4 on Windows 10

Raspberry Pi 4 can run on Windows, but incidentally, not the full desktop version of Windows 10 that you and I are conversant with. Instead, the Pi 3 runs on Windows 10 IoT Core, i.e., a reduced version of Windows 10 that doesn't boot entirely into the graphical desktop and is planned to be managed via a command-line interface on a remote computer. It can merely run a sole full-screen Universal Windows Platform app at one time, for example, a kiosk app for retail shops, even though other software can run in the background.

Nevertheless, the Pi can function as a Windows 10 thin client, wherever Windows 10 is run on a server and streamed to the Pi, and, with a dominant sufficient server, the experience can be virtually the same as running a Windows 10 PC. With the added power of the Pi 4, together with its dual-display support, the Pi is likely to make a further incursion into the thin client market.

The Pi 4 also is likely to have the power to run a full desktop version of Windows on Arm, but it is with

Microsoft to make any decision to port Windows to the Pi 4.

Raspberry Pi 4 running on windows 10 desktop apps

The Pi 4 can function with Windows desktop apps, although it requires a considerable effort to be successful; even so, the apps will only run weakly.

It used to be possible to do so utilizing the ExaGear Desktop software, although this is no longer available for sale. However, there are free alternatives, such as Pi386.

Whichever way you want to adopt, performance will be below par, since the tools considered necessary to run Windows apps on the Pi require so much processing power that you're principally limited to running 20-year-old Windows apps and games, and simple modern text editors.

Finally, while it's in principle possible, it's not something to be recommended.

CHAPTER EIGHT

Getting the most from your Raspberry Pi 4

It makes economic sense to invest in a case to protect the Pi from damage, particularly if you're going to be moving the Pi with you. But don't forget before you invest in a case that the Pi 4 doesn't fit earlier Pi cases as a result of a change in its layout.

It also makes sense to shell out for a high-speed micro SD card, as outlined below, if effectiveness is vital to you.

The Pi can run many operating systems, if you're concerned about stability and excellent performance then the official Raspbian operating system is the best selection; having decided to get the most from the Pi, and having been provided with a fast web browser and a decent range of office and programming software.

If you didn't install the Raspbian OS using the NOOBS installer, and perhaps you're running out of space: you can navigate to the terminal and input 'sudo raspi-config' and then choose the option to "Enlarge root partition to fill SD card,' this will ensure you're using the allocated space on the card

Roadmap for Ubuntu official support for the Raspberry Pi 4

With the October 2019 official release of Ubuntu Server, Canonical declared formal support for the Raspberry Pi 4. The most recent board from the Raspberry Pi Foundation sports a quicker system-on-a-chip with a processor that supports the Cortex-A72 architecture (quad-core 64-bit ARMv8 at 1.5GHz). Moreover, it puts forward up to 4GB of RAM. "We are supporting the

Raspberry Pi 4 to give developers access to a low-cost board, powerful enough to consolidate computer workloads at the edge".

The Raspberry Pi is now reputed as a most easily reached platform for innovators in the implanted space. Canonical is committed to authorizing innovators with open-source software. As a result, Canonical tries to provide full official support for all the boards in the Raspberry Pi family. Canonical will, therefore, allow both Ubuntu Server and Ubuntu Core for both the current and future Pi boards.

The Raspberry Pi, 4 Model B, is offered with different selections of RAM: 1GB, 2GB and 4GB. However, Canonical official support for this board is presently restricted to the 1GB and 2GB versions. This is as a result of a kernel bug; USB ports are not shored up out of the box in the official arm64 image on the 4GB RAM version. Canonical engineers have identified kernel repairs. We are presently testing these fixes broadly. We will provide updates within a space of weeks following successful tests...

Canonical has therefore asked developers to use a temporary workaround to facilitate USB on the

4GB RAM version. The provisional solution will include the editing of the file /boot/firmware/usercfg.txt to limit RAM to 3GB, as follows:

total_mem=3072

Getting help with the Raspberry Pi 4

Help is available with the Raspberry P 14. With over 27 million boards sold since the first Pi debut in 2012, the board can now boast of a strong community, which helps other users through the official Raspberry Pi site and forums.

Keeping the Raspberry Pi 4 up-dated

If you're using the Pi's official Raspbian operating system, then keeping the Pi up to date is relatively easy. You will be guided on how to get your firmware updates

You can get the latest update firmware for your Raspberry Pi by following these instructions:

• 	Step 1: Be sure you are connected to the Web.

To ensure that your Raspberry Pi 4 has internet connectivity either via Wi-Fi or you have a network cable plugged in.

This can be verified by making sure your Raspberry Pi 4 can open any links on the browser.

• Step 2: Open a Terminal Window

Opening a terminal window from the taskbar or application menu will get you ready for updates.

• Step 3: Perform update on Terminal window

You will first update your system package list by entering this following command: Sudo apt update

When this is done, you will need to type in this following command to update all your installed app packages to their latest versions: sudo apt full-upgrade

- Step 4: Reboot your Raspberry Pi 4

o After the upgrade has finished downloading and installed, you will need to restart your Raspberry Pi 4 by typing in the following command:

sudo shutdown - r now

And you're finished. You have just got yourself the latest firmware for Raspberry Pi

CHAPTER NINE

Raspberry kits availability

Raspberry Pi 4 Details and stock/availability at most retail stores

The incredible Raspberry Pi board has developed again! Model 4B is now the latest product, and it includes several upgrades that are important enough to place the Pi 4 as a desktop replacement. Here is all the information available about the new boards (there are three editions!), the new features, and what relevant part you might need because of the modifications.

New Features and Upgrades

The most unanticipated modification for the Pi 4B is that it is offered with three variations of speed DDR4 SDRAM memory; 1GB, 2GB, or 4GB. Combined with a newer 1.5GHz quad-core processor, the Pi 4B can accommodate a higher number of programs and tasks faster than ever before.

Communications have been upgraded to current standards; Bluetooth 5.0, USB 3.0 (two ports), and true Gigabit Ethernet for fast communication through wireless and wired interfaces. The twin-band wireless LAN now includes modular compliance certification, letting the board to be designed into end products with abridged compliance testing, getting better on both cost and time.

Video output has altered considerably with the Pi 4B. Twin micro-HDMI ports letting the following show configurations:

- One show at 4Kp60 resolution

- Two shows at 1080p60 resolution

- "probably" two shows at 4Kp30 resolution

With 4K resolution and twin monitor support, the Pi 4B is a tough player for many applications, such as desktop stand-in, media hub, and digital signage. The micro-HDMI will employ the use of an adapter or adapting cable to hook up to most displays.

A boost in the power input has been made, permitting 3.0A of existing instead of 2.5A through a new USB-C connector. Power supplies for the Pi are also currently available with native USB-C connectors, but earlier 2.5A models can be applied effectively with adapters.

Availability

Most of the latest Pi 4 products are now available from the date of their launching announcement. Initial quantities were limited, which is usual for the release of new Pi boards and accessories. But today, they are readily available in all retail stores handling the Raspberry Pi products.

What You'll Need

With new board models, some items have become incompatible and require to be replaced. Here's a list of things that you'll need if you purchase a Pi 4B board. Note that these are included in many of the kits, and that you can save a bit of money by buying them in kit form

i.   Raspberry Pi 4B Budget Kit

ii.   Raspberry Pi 4 B Starter Kit

iii.   Raspberry Pi 4 Model B/1GB

iv.   Raspberry Pi 4 Model B/2GB

v.   Raspberry Pi 4 Model B/4GB

vi.   Class 10 16GB MicroSD Card with Raspbian (Stretch)

vii.   High Pi Raspberry Pi Case for Pi 4

viii.   Micro-HDMI to Standard HDMI (A/M), 1m cable

ix.   Micro-HDMI-HDM Adapter

Which Micro SD card and size for Raspberry Pi 4

Micro-SD card: A formatted Micro SD card will be needed to make storing of files and the Raspbian Operating

System possible. 8 GB is, in fact, the minimum storage prerequisite, but you should need more than that. Get a 16 GB or more so that you have enough to play with. Better still, you may have your Raspberry Pi 4 pre-installed with the Raspberry Operating System so that you don't need further works before you are ready to start using the system.

CHAPTER TEN

Connecting Raspberry Pi 4 to Wi-Fi

If you are using the Raspberry Pi 4 or older versions with a screen, keyboard, a mouse, and the compatible apps installed, you can navigate and click the wireless symbol in the top-right-hand corner of the Pi's desktop.

A dropdown menu will show up, letting you select your network. On the Raspberry Pi 3B+, a country should be selected too for regulatory reasons before you can effectively make a connection.

On the other hand, you can make use of Raspi-Config if you have a keyboard and a display attached to your Pi or if you have configured SSH. Whichever way, you can carry out the Raspi-Config application, which is a very plain graphical user interface that lets you modify various settings.

Using the Command Line

The command-line approach is the most sophisticated method. However, once it's configured, it is also the most adaptable method. Besides, you can even classify numerous networking profiles. Just like above, this approach can be used to set-up your Raspberry Pi remotely.

Headless Wi-Fi Set-up

So far, all the methods mentioned require you to have some access to the Raspberry Pi you want to configure. However, if you're going to use the system without peripherals, you wouldn't like to connect it through an Ethernet cable; you can position a configuration file in the boot directory of a newly created SD card. When the Pi boots initially, the

Wi-Fi network is configured automatically. This procedure can also be adapted to apply to SSH.

Setup over Bluetooth

If you have an Android device, you can apply the method illustrated in Connecting Raspberry Pi 3 Wi-Fi Via Bluetooth to hook up your Raspberry Pi to a Wi-Fi network. Mostly, the Pi uses a Python script that carries out the necessary commands, the same way you would physically use it when it gets the command to do so by an Android app.

Although going through the steps in the article, you can create your solution that runs in a web browser

as a substitute for an Android app.

CHAPTER ELEVEN

Networking with Raspberry Pi 4

 You can run a network of Raspberry Pi4, running, and updating the boards should be made easy by the capability to boot from a network-attached file system utilizing PXE, allowing admins to share operating system images between machines. An upcoming firmware update will add PXE backing to the Pi 4.king with Raspberry Pi 4

Raspberry Pi4 on 64-bit

Raspberry Pi 4 is a 64-bit board. But the benefits are restricted to the 64-bit processor, outside of a few more operating systems possibly being able to run on the Pi.

Rather than marketing a 64-bit version of the official Raspbian operating system, the Raspberry Pi Foundation has announced it would concentrate on optimizing the Pi's official Raspbian OS for 32-bit performance to accommodate the needs of the millions of older, 32-bit Pi boards that have already been sold.

Raspberry Pi just a motherboard

Raspberry is a motherboard with the lowest price tag of $35, although there are different types of kits available that if packaged together, attract higher prices, along with a case, leads and electronics for getting started with -- all for an additional cost, of course. This £70 official Raspberry Pi 4 starter packaged kit, much of what you need, including a case, bar the screen, keyboard and mouse.

Who makes the Raspberry Pi?

The Raspberry Pi boards are invented by a subsidiary company of the Raspberry Pi Foundation, a charitable organization devoted to promoting computer science education, and produce at a Sony factory in South Wales. Since its inception, the Pi has been approved by many schools, and its availability has also coincided with an almost increasing threefold in the number of people applying to study computer science at Cambridge.

The foundation's initiator and board co-creator Eben Upton is understood to have said he began designing the board in an attempt to encourage children to be trained in computing, after being hit by how few people were applying to study computer science at Cambridge during the middle of 2000

CHAPTER TWELVE

Speech recognition with Raspberry Pi 4

The Raspberry Pi 4 can carry out speech recognition utilizing a well-known open-source option, known as Jasper, which can be installed on the Pi and used even in the absence of an internet connection.

Most selections for speech recognition rely on a cloud service. Hence it requires an internet connection, such as Google Speech or Alexa Voice Service.

An easy way to add speech recognition to the Pi is via Google's Voice AIY (Artificial Inteligence yourself) kit, which provides all the extra hardware needed to turn the Pi into a Google Voice assistant.

How to build a cluster of Raspberry Pi 4 boards

A cluster of Raspberry Pi 4 can be built certainly, one moderately low-cost choice is to merge eight boards into an OctaPi cluster. When combined, the power is far faster than a board on its own when calculating prime factors, a crucial task when cracking encryption.

At the farthest end of the scale is this 750 Pi cluster that has been put together at the Los Alamos National Laboratory, and which is due to measuring up to 10,000 boards in the future.

Training a neural network with the Raspberry Pi 4

Neural network training cannot be done using Raspberry because it is not powerful enough to train neural networks to do anything constructive. It is recommended that you use a better, more robust computer with a mid to high-end graphics processing capability (GPU) or an out-and-out cloud computing instance, such as an AWS P3 or a Google Cloud Platform Cloud TPU (Tensor Processing Unit) instance.

Running a neural network on Raspberry Pi 4

A neural network and machine learning can be done on Raspberry Pi 4, but you are likely to procure some additional hardware if you want it to be effective. For instance, Google's Coral USB sticks, which pick up at the pace and rate at which the Pi can transmit vision-related tasks, like facial and object recognition, using its specialized cores. It can speed up machine-

learning models built via Google's
TensorFlow Lite library

CHAPTER THIRTEEN

How to set up a printer on Raspberry Pi

I. Get Pi Installation up and running.

    In the first place, do ensure your Pi Raspbian installation is running as necessary, and no background programs are running on your systems. Also, make sure you have internet connections. All these set, open up a new terminal window by clicking LXTerminal.

II. Install CUPS

Install CUPS using APT

III. Install Nano

Install Nano via APT. Nano is a text editor that runs from within a terminal window.

IV. Edit config

Edit the CUPS config files to make sure they are set to make the printer accessible over the network. Once that is carried out, reboot the server.

V. Access locally

On the Pi, open a browser and go to the address below. 'Add printer is a choice you make next. When prompted, key in your surname and password. View the network printers shown on the list.

VI. Test the printer

To test run the print page, click on 'administration,' then 'manage printers' View your printer listed. Click on the name of the printer to see more information about the printer. Then choose 'print

test page' from the
maintenance drop-down
menu

CONCLUSION

The introduction of Raspberry Pi in 2012 was a giant leap towards the mass education of the children folk in computing and programming. Since 2012, there have been different versions of the Pi 2, Pi4, with RAM 1, 2, 4. The Raspberry Pi 4 can serve as a desktop with almost similar functions but with considerable price advantage

As has been said, the new Raspberry Pi 4, Model B, is offered in three variants. The bottom priced version is built with the same 1GB of memory as all the earlier models and are priced the same at $35. The second variant is available with 2GB RAM priced at $45, and at a high end is the model 4GB of RAM, priced at $55. But there aren't any other disparities between the three models apart from the amount of RAM on the board.

Up until now, competitors have come up with versions with extra memory, Gigabit Ethernet, or USB 3, but so far, no headway in terms of competing favorably has been made. On the price front, competitors are yet to wage war.

ABOUT THE AUTHOR

Louis Gomera is a graduate in communication and a geek for more than three years, although he has been writing about Apple for many years, he also shares useful tips through his books to help readers use their Apps efficiently and effectively. Louis is a lover of audiovisual elements, creative, a fan of photography and cinema, and knows how to make every moment a story. As a die-hard fan of Apple, he loves writing and giving audiences unique, unexpected and latest updates in the Tech world. He has already helped a lot of people change their habits to improve at all levels and be more productive with their iPhone and other smart gadgets.

INDEX

Made in the USA
Monee, IL
29 November 2020